D1451353

HURRICANES

Dean Galiano

the rosen publishing group's
rosen central
new york

Published in 2000 by The Rosen Publishing Group, Inc.
29 East 21st Street, New York, NY 10010

First Edition

Galiano, Dean.
     Hurricanes / by Dean Galiano.
        p. cm. — (Weather watchers' library)
     Includes bibliographical references and index.
     Summary: Examines the development, structure, destructive capabilities, and significance of hurricanes. Includes a chapter on hurricane prediction and safety.
     ISBN 0-8239-3095-5
     1. Hurricanes Juvenile literature. [1. Hurricanes.] I. Title. II. Series: Galiano, Dean. Weather watchers' library.
     QC944.2.G35 1999
     551.55'2—dc21   99-35636
                                  CIP

Manufactured in the United States of America

CONTENTS

Introduction 4

1 The Birth of a Hurricane 7

2 Hurricane Structure 19

3 Hurricane Destruction 27

4 Hurricane Prediction and
   Safety 35

   Glossary 42

   For Further Reading 44

   Resources 45

   Index 46

Introduction

Hurricanes are one of the most damaging and deadly kinds of extreme weather. Hurricanes are powerful storms that form over warm tropical oceans. When a hurricane reaches the shore, it brings with it torrential rains and flooding, strong winds, high waves, and even tornadoes. These forces combine to result in incredible destruction.

Hurricanes strike the United States on an average of five times every three years, with Florida receiving most of the hits. Hurricanes are very costly, both in terms of human life and in property damage.

Hurricane Andrew was the most expensive natural disaster in the history of the United States. On August 24, 1992, Hurricane Andrew tore its way across southern Florida, leaving behind a path of destruction. Winds gusting to speeds of 165 miles per hour destroyed homes and businesses, leaving fifty-three people dead and 180,000 homeless. The total cost of damages was estimated at 25 billion dollars. Two days later, Andrew racked up another 400 million dollars in damages as it plowed into the Louisiana coast.

4

High winds and flooding contribute to a hurricane's destructive power.

1 The Birth of a Hurricane

There are many types of severe storms, but none so dangerous as a hurricane. Whereas a tornado is also a powerful, rotating storm, hurricanes can last longer and carry far more energy than tornadoes. In fact, the average hurricane releases so much energy, it is equal to the annual production of electricity for the entire United States!

What Is a Hurricane?

A hurricane is a large, tightly coiled storm that is a type of tropical cyclone. Tropical cyclones are weather systems that form over the warm waters of tropical oceans, usually in late summer or early fall. All tropical cyclones have a recognizable cyclonic, or circular, spinning motion. In a hurricane, strong winds swirl around the storm's calm center, called the eye. This formation gives a hurricane its spiral appearance.

Hurricanes can destroy entire communities.

For a tropical cyclone to be called a hurricane, it must have wind speeds of at least 74 miles per hour. The whole storm system may be anywhere from five to six miles high and 300 to 600 miles across, about the width of 400 football fields. It moves like a giant spinning top, traveling forward at speeds of about fifteen miles per hour.

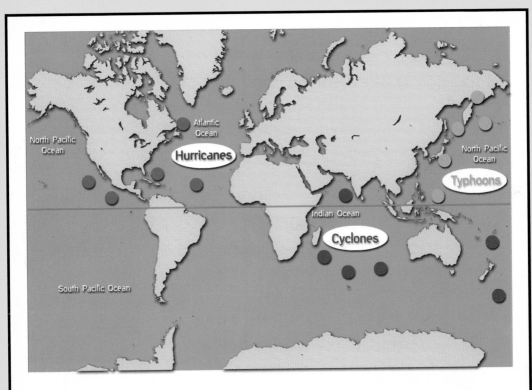

Depending on the ocean region, a tropical cyclone can be called a hurricane, a typhoon, or a cyclone.

Tropical cyclones of this size and strength in the Atlantic Ocean are known as hurricanes, in the western and north Pacific Ocean as typhoons, and in the Indian and south Pacific Oceans as cyclones.

The Life Cycle of Tropical Storms

Tropical storms do not start out as hurricanes. Over time, they develop and grow in strength. The first signal that a hurricane may be forming is the appearance over tropical seas of a cluster of thunderclouds (clouds that usually produce storms). If this cluster has a center of low pressure, it is called a tropical disturbance. Low pressure areas form when lighter, warmer air rises above heavier, colder air, creating unstable weather conditions.

If the air pressure in a tropical disturbance begins to fall, and winds begin moving in a cyclonic motion, the storm becomes a tropical depression. A tropical depression is a type of tropical cyclone. Tropical cyclone classifications are based on ten minutes of sustained, or constant, wind speeds during a storm. In a tropical depression, the maximum sustained wind speed is 38 miles per hour.

Should winds begin circling more quickly around the low-pressure center of a tropical depression, the system is upgraded to a tropical storm. A tropical

9

storm has maximum sustained wind speeds of 39 to 73 miles per hour. For a storm system to be called a hurricane, sustained wind speeds must reach or exceed 74 miles per hour.

Conditions for Hurricane Development

Three conditions must be present for hurricane formation: warm-surface ocean waters, high humidity (moisture in the air), and cyclonic (spiraling) wind patterns. A hurricane forms when air comes into contact with warm ocean waters. It then gathers additional heat and energy from the moisture contained in humid air. The heat causes a low-pressure system to develop, creating thunderstorms and strong cyclonic surface winds. These winds produce stormy seas, pulling the warm, moist air upward and inward in a circling motion. In turn, this moisture produces more heat and energy, and the storm begins to feed on itself. A hurricane is born!

How Hurricanes Develop

A hurricane requires warm, humid conditions to develop, and strong winds and moist air to keep going. A hurricane begins to form when air comes in contact with warm ocean waters and begins

The Coriolis Effect

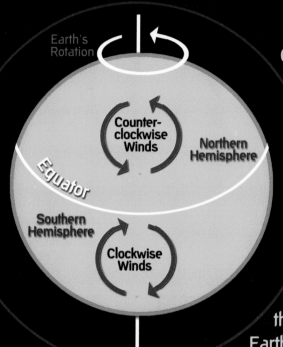

Cyclonic motion, which sets off circulation in a storm system, is caused by a force called the Coriolis effect. The spinning of the earth creates the Coriolis force, which is the curving of the wind that blows through Earth's atmosphere. The wind in the Northern Hemisphere (north of the equator) curves to the right, whereas the wind in the Southern Hemisphere (south of the equator) curves to the left.

Because hurricanes form in the Northern Hemisphere, their winds rotate in a counter-clockwise direction. The opposite occurs in storms forming in the Southern Hemisphere, where the wind has a clockwise rotation.

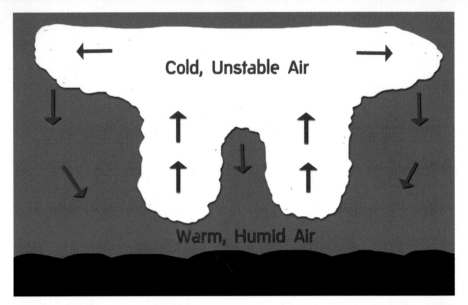

Cold, Unstable Air

Warm, Humid Air

As a tropical storm develops, it pulls in warm, moist air from the ocean surface. The rising air creates unstable conditions that lead to thunderstorm formation.

rising in temperature. If sea-surface temperatures are at least 80 degrees, the storm will be supplied with enough heat to develop into a hurricane. As water vapor evaporates from the ocean surface, it condenses, or turns from vapor to liquid. With condensation, clouds and rain begin to form. As the water vapor condenses, it releases heat. Since warm air is lighter than cool air, the heated air begins to rise. This causes temperatures in the core of the storm to increase, making air rise even higher.

The movement of air, along with rising storm

temperatures, causes a sharp drop in air pressure. As air from the high-pressure zone above the storm rushes in to fill the area of low pressure, winds begin to form. The greater the difference in pressure between the high and low areas, the stronger the wind. Due to the Coriolis effect, these strong winds start rotating in a counterclockwise motion near the ocean surface. The winds stir up the ocean, sending moist air spiraling upward and inward toward the center of the storm. As the moist, heated air reaches the storm's center, the system builds up momentum and begins to spin faster. The spiraling winds gain speed as they approach the center of the storm, like a whirlpool.

As the hurricane develops, it continues to draw warm, moist air from lower regions and begins to exhaust (blow out) cooler air at the top. Without this outlet at the top of the storm, the hurricane's center would fill up with air. If the center fills up, the difference in air pressure between the center of the storm and the edges of the storm will decrease, and the storm will soon die out. The effect would be somewhat like a vacuum cleaner with a full bag. When the bag is full, the vacuum cleaner has less sucking power. Replacing the full bag with an empty bag makes more room for the inrushing air.

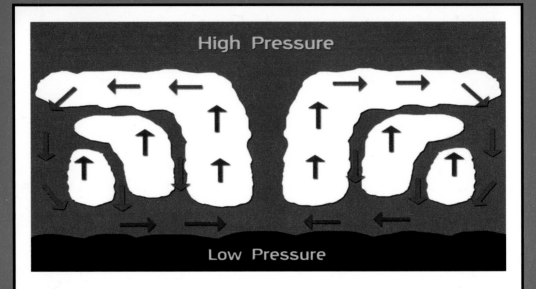

High Pressure

Low Pressure

A hurricane sucks in warm, moist air near the ocean surface and exhausts cool, dry air at its top. This results in areas of low and high pressure, which create the storm's strong winds.

When upward-moving air is released at the top of the storm, it creates an area of low pressure in the center of the storm. This low-pressure area in effect empties the center of the storm. To fill up the area of low pressure, air is sucked in from below. The storm will continue this cycle of drawing in and exhausting air as long as cyclonic wind movement and warm, moist conditions are present.

This upward movement of moist air, along with the low-pressure center, produces bands of thunderstorms. These thunderstorms allow the air to

Anatomy of a Hurricane

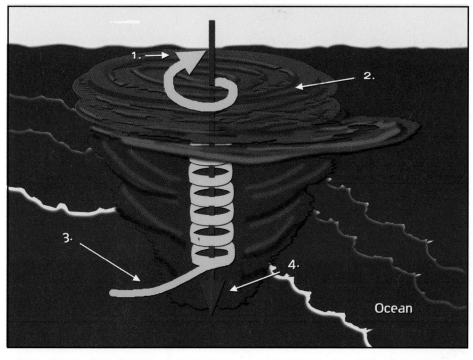

Ocean

1. **Exhaust** Upward-moving air is blown out at the top of the hurricane.
2. **Thunderstorms** Spiraling warm, moist air produces bands of thunderstorms.
3. **Eye** Cool air descends, creating an area of low pressure and calm weather at the storm's center.
4. **Spiraling Winds** Warm, moist air is sucked in from the ocean's surface to fill the area of low pressure. The air swirls and rises around this center, creating a column of rapidly spinning wind.

grow warmer and rise higher into the atmosphere, to heights of 30,000 feet or above. If the winds at this height are light, and the winds at all levels of the storm are blowing in the same direction, the column of air will maintain its shape, grow stronger, and become a hurricane.

2000

Albert	Debby	Gordon	Joyce
Beryl	Ernesto	Helene	Keith
Chris	Florence	Isaac	

2001

Allison	Dean	Gabrielle	Jerry
Barry	Erin	Humberto	Karen
Chantal	Felix	Iris	

Naming Hurricanes

When a weather system in the United States develops into a tropical storm, the National Weather Service gives it a name from an alphabetical list prepared each year. When a tropical storm becomes a hurricane, it keeps its name. From 1953 to 1978, tropical storms were given only women's names. In 1979, men's names began to be used as well.

Since hurricanes affect many nations and cultures, the World Meteorological Association also gives storms international names. Many of these names are recycled throughout the years. However, when a hurricane is very destructive and memorable, its name is retired. Here is the list of names for tropical storms and hurricanes of the Atlantic Ocean for 2000–2001.

Lorenzo   Olga   Sebastien   Wendy
Michelle   Pablo   Tanya
Noel   Rebekah   Van

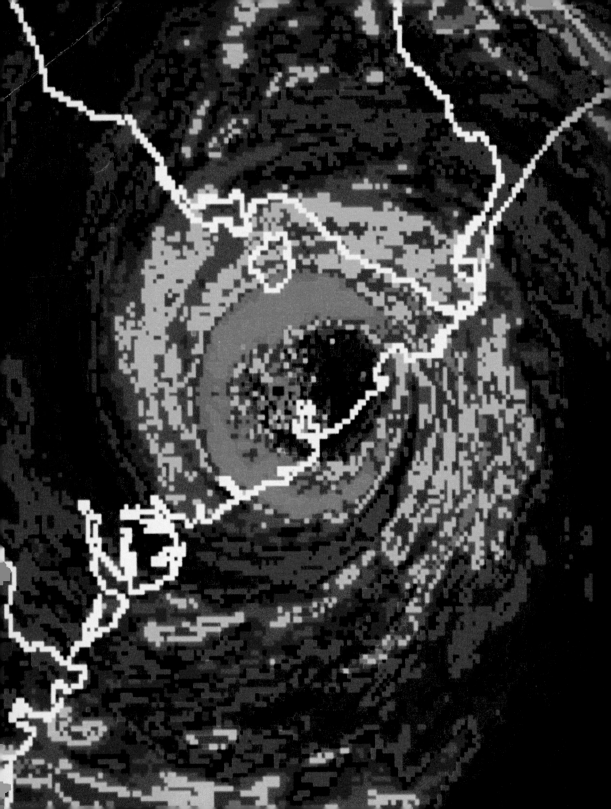

2 Hurricane Structure

Hurricanes are highly organized storms. They consist of three distinct parts: the eye, the eye wall, and spiral rainbands. These parts combine to give the hurricane its unique appearance.

The Eye of the Hurricane

If you could slice a hurricane down the middle and look at its structure, you would notice a clear, calm core surrounded by violent activity. This core is called the eye. Hurricanes are the only storms that have an eye. The eye is an area of very low air pressure that is usually about 20 to 30 miles across, though some eyes have been measured at 70 to 90 miles across. Not all eyes are circular in shape; some are oblong, stretching out in the direction that the hurricane is moving.

The temperatures in the eye are much warmer than outside it. There is also very little moisture

This radar picture shows a hurricane's three distinctive parts. The spiral rainbands are yellow and green, the eye wall is red, and the calm eye of the storm is black.

19

Caught in the Eye

There are many strange events associated with the eye of a hurricane. Perhaps the oddest of these is the sight of large numbers of birds attempting to ride out the storm in the safety of the eye. Because of the ferocious winds surrounding the eye, the birds cannot fly out of this calm center. They are then forced to travel with the storm. The eye often contains many birds that are not familiar to observers on the ground. At times, tropical birds have ended up in New England—more than 2,000 miles from their normal habitat!

found in the eye, so it is almost cloud-free. As a result, when the eye passes over a region, there is a lull, or break, in the storm, and the weather becomes calm. Depending on how big the hurricane is, the calm weather may last from a few minutes to several hours.

During the lull, many people mistakenly think that the hurricane is over. Such an occurrence took place in Miami, Florida, in 1926. When the eye of a powerful hurricane passed over the Miami area, people thought the storm had ended. They went outdoors and looked at the damage that the hurricane had caused. Despite warnings, many people stayed outside, and some even went swimming! Before long, the other side of the storm bore down on the area. Swimmers were dragged out to sea to their deaths. As cars crossed over the causeway, high waves swept them into the ocean. In all, there were a total of 243 deaths, most of them due to drowning.

The Eye Wall and Spiral Rainbands

Surrounding the eye of the hurricane are towering walls of rotating thunderclouds, making up the eye wall. This is where the heaviest rains fall and the strongest winds occur, because the clouds are concentrated around the low-pressure area. The bases of these clouds are usually about 500 feet above the ground, and they extend upward 40,000 to 50,000 feet. Spinning outward from the eye wall are spiral rainbands, bands of clouds accompanied by heavy rainshowers and hurricane-force winds. At the farthest edges of the storm, circling the spiral rainbands, are high, thin cirrus clouds. Rain and winds are fairly light in this cloud area.

Wind Speeds

The clouds and winds associated with hurricanes normally extend outward from the eye about 100 to 450 miles. At the outer edges of the storm, rains are light, and wind speeds are only about 35 miles per hour. As you move toward the eye, rainfall amounts will vary, and wind speeds will steadily increase. Within about 30 miles of the eye, in the eye wall, the strongest winds are found. Wind speeds here reach as high as 100 to 150 miles per hour. In some instances, wind speeds have been estimated at more than 200 miles per hour, faster than many tornadoes.

Hurricane Movement

A typical hurricane moves from east to west because of the tropical trade winds that blow near the equator. Trade winds in the Northern Hemisphere (north of the equator) blow from the East, carrying the moisture that hurricanes need to develop. Eventually, a developing hurricane will move northward into a region of winds known as the prevailing westerlies. These winds direct hurricanes north and then eastward. The typical path of a hurricane is C-shaped, with the open end of the C facing east. This combination of directional winds is known as steering winds. The direction of these winds depends on the location of areas of high and low pressure near the storm.

When the steering winds are strong, it is easier

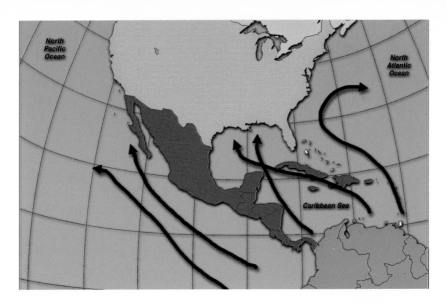

Trade winds in the Northern Hemisphere blow hurricanes westward. As hurricanes move north, some are caught by westerly winds and begin to circle back eastward.

for scientists to predict a hurricane's path—it is usually east to west and then northward. When the steering winds are weak, however, hurricane movement is more difficult to predict. Hurricanes may zigzag, reverse direction, or follow erratic (irregular) paths.

Although wind speeds within a hurricane reach 74 miles per hour or more, the storm system itself moves forward at only about 10 to 30 miles per hour. In the early stages of development, hurricanes move slowly—less than 20 miles per hour. As a typical hurricane grows in strength, it begins to curve away from the equator. This happens because the Coriolis effect causes the wind to curve, pushing the hurricane northeast. The hurricane gains speed in these winds and begins moving at about 20 to 30 miles per hour. Occasionally, hurricanes move forward at speeds of up to 60 miles per hour.

The Death of a Hurricane

A hurricane can be viewed as a giant engine that must be fed a steady stream of fuel to keep it going. The fuel for a hurricane is warm, moist air. When a hurricane moves inland, its energy supply is cut off, and the hurricane begins losing its strength. Unlike warm ocean water, land cannot provide the hurricane with the necessary moisture. Contact with land also slows the storm's winds. The hurricane's eye wall weakens, the winds stop their spinning motion—a process called spin down—and the hurricane breaks apart.

Even the death of a hurricane can give rise to violent weather. Damage and loss of life can extend hundreds of miles inland. As a hurricane spins down, it carries large amounts of moist air, producing heavy rains that often lead to flash flooding. Tornadoes also can spin off from a hurricane's fierce winds.

Heavy rain from hurricanes can cause flash flooding.

3 Hurricane Destruction

When a hurricane reaches land, a number of factors contribute to its destructive capabilities. In addition to strong winds, hurricanes can produce heavy rains, severe flooding, and deadly storm surges—huge domes of ocean water that flood coastal areas.

Wind Damage

Winds within a hurricane travel at such high speeds that a hurricane's energy may be up to 12,000 times more powerful than that of an ordinary storm. These wind speeds range from a low of 74 miles per hour to over 200 miles per hour. As wind speeds increase, the damage inflicted by the winds also increases.

Even during the weakest hurricanes, winds can severely damage buildings and mobile homes. When wind speeds reach 125 to 200 miles per hour, the effect is far more destructive. For example, when

Hurricanes produce dangerous storm surges.

Hurricane Andrew plowed ashore in South Florida during the early morning of August 24, 1992, estimated wind speeds were 145 miles per hour with gusts to 175 miles per hour. Telephone poles and trees were tossed about like twigs. The storm tore entire rooftops loose from buildings and sent them bouncing down the streets like hats caught up on a windy day. Loose debris, such as house siding, furniture, and road signs, flew through the air at such great speed that they became deadly missiles.

Flooding

In addition to the destruction caused by powerful winds, hurricanes also produce dangerously heavy rains. Even after hurricanes move inland and begin to lose their strength, heavy rains—often six inches or more—cause deadly, destructive flooding. In June 1972, Hurricane Agnes dropped large amounts of rain from Virginia to New England. This heavy rainfall caused many rivers to spill over their banks. The rising water forced more than 250,000 people to flee from their homes. Almost half of the deaths caused by this hurricane were related to flooding.

Storm Surges

Storm surges created by hurricanes can be more

threatening to life and property than the storm's strong winds and heavy rains. A storm surge is a 50- to 100-mile-wide dome of ocean water—sometimes topped by waves—created by a combination of hurricane-force winds, high tides, and low pressure. When a storm surge hits, it destroys marinas, beach homes, and other shoreline structures. It also washes away beaches, coastal roads, and railway beds.

A tragic example of a coastal community being destroyed by surging ocean waters occurred at the turn of the century. On the morning of September 8, 1900, a deadly storm swept across the Gulf of Mexico, battering the island city of Galveston, Texas. Much of the city was less than ten feet above sea level; the highest land was only about fifteen feet above sea level. By noon, storm surges had flooded the waterfront area and the streets of the city. Water submerged bridges and train tracks connecting Galveston to the mainland, cutting off any possible escape route. At 2:30 PM, half of the city was underwater. The water rose so rapidly that by 5:00 PM, the entire city was submerged under fifteen feet of water. Homes, rooftops, trees, and chunks of stone from buildings crashed into the flooded streets. Rushing waters became clogged with wreckage, pinning residents underwater to

Galveston before the hurricane of 1900

drown. As people tried to escape to higher ground, they were injured or killed by debris that was being driven by 120-mile-per-hour winds.

When the waters had finally receded, over half of Galveston had been totally destroyed. The rest of the city had sustained severe damage. It is estimated that more than 6,000 people lost their lives. This hurricane is the worst U.S. weather disaster on record.

The survivors of the Galveston storm had to make an important decision: move, or stay and rebuild the city. Those who chose to stay not only rebuilt the city, but also constructed a huge seawall. This 17-foot-high wall was designed to

Storm surges can be over twenty feet high.

keep out the giant waves and storm surges produced by hurricanes. The seawall helped protect Galveston when a similar hurricane hit in 1915.

Hurricane Strength

Scientists measure a hurricane's strength using the Saffir-Simpson scale. It rates the intensity of hurricanes on a scale of 1 to 5, with 1 being the least destructive and 5 being the most destructive. Each category indicates 1) maximum wind speed, 2) height of the storm surge, and 3) the amount of damage done. Category 3, 4, and 5 storms are considered major hurricanes. Although only 21 percent of hurricanes that strike the United States are major hurricanes, they account for over 83 percent of the hurricane damage in the United States.

The potential for property damage rises rapidly with a hurricane's ranking on the Saffir-Simpson scale. A Category 2 hurricane has ten times the amount of destructive power of a Category 1 hurricane, while a Category 4 or 5 storm can inflict 100 to 250 times more damage!

Saffir-Simpson Scale

Category	Maximum Wind Speed (mph)	Storm Surge Height (feet)	Damage
1	74−95	4−5	Minimal
2	96−110	6−8	Moderate
3	111−130	9−12	Extensive
4	131−155	13−18	Extreme
5	156+	19+	Catastrophic

4 Hurricane Prediction and Safety

The 1998 hurricane season was one of the most destructive on record. It was an extremely active season, with seven tropical storms or hurricanes hitting the United States—more than twice the yearly average. These storms also racked up more than 6.5 billion dollars in damages. According to forecasters, the 1999 hurricane season promises to be every bit as damaging as the previous year.

Since people continue to live in areas subject to hurricane destruction, it is up to scientists to help keep them safe. Scientists have been studying ways to try to slow down or stop a hurricane. Unfortunately, these methods have not proved to be successful. With advances in computer and satellite technology, scientists have improved their ability to track a hurricane by two percent or better each year. Today's forecasts are far more reliable than they were even five years ago.

Advances in technology, such as the Doppler radar, have improved our ability to track hurricanes.

Improvements in Technology

Weather forecasters use a number of different kinds of technology to track the movement of hurricanes, including weather satellites, computers, and radar. Forecasts have become more accurate as the technology becomes more sophisticated. Satellites 22,000 miles above Earth measure temperature, winds, moisture, and cloud cover in the atmosphere. This data is transmitted every half hour to weather services around the globe. Meteorologists (scientists who study weather) use this information, along with computer models, to make predictions about a hurricane's movements. It is important that forecasters know where a hurricane will strike so they can evacuate (order people to leave) a region, if necessary. Forecasters also try to predict when a hurricane will come ashore to determine how much time people will have to leave. Since evacuation costs about one million dollars per mile of coastline, the more accurate the forecasts, the less money will need to be spent.

It can be difficult to predict where a hurricane will strike because hurricanes may follow very erratic paths. Forecasters may also have difficulty judging the weather conditions inside the hurricane. Knowing those conditions can help forecasters determine the strength of a storm. It also helps them to better predict the path that a hurricane will take.

One way to retrieve this information is to send airplanes out to fly through the storm. The people who fly these planes are called Hurricane Hunters.

Hurricane Hunters

Members of the Air Force Reserve's 53rd Weather Reconnaissance Squadron are the official Hurricane Hunters. During each mission, the Hurricane Hunters fly several times into the eye of the hurricane to record weather conditions. They locate the exact center of the hurricane and determine whether the storm is growing stronger or weaker. Throughout the flight, instruments on the plane record wind speed and direction. This data is useful in forecasting the

Hurricane Hunters record weather data from inside the eye of a hurricane.

path that the hurricane will take. The information gathered by the Hurricane Hunters helps meteorologists improve their forecasts by up to 30 percent.

Hurricane Safety

Hurricanes are dangerous, even deadly. However, the threat of destruction has not kept people from living in areas that experience the most hurricane activity. About 45 million people live along the United States' hurricane-prone coastline, and many others move there each year. For example, Florida—the state most affected by hurricanes—leads the nation in population growth.

If you live in an area where hurricane activity takes place, you and your family should always be prepared. Take some time to plan an evacuation route. Contact your local emergency management office or American Red Cross chapter and ask for the community hurricane preparedness plan. This plan will show you the safest evacuation routes and the locations of nearby hurricane shelters. If you have pets, be sure to find out if they are allowed at area hurricane shelters. If they are not, your local humane society can give you information on nearby animal shelters.

Your family should also develop an emergency

communication plan. This will help if family members become separated from one another during a hurricane. Ask an out-of-state relative or friend to be a family contact so that you and your family will be able to locate one another after the storm. Be sure that each family member knows the contact person's phone number and address.

Everyone in your family should also know how to:

⊙ Turn off your home's gas, electricity, and water
⊙ Call 911
⊙ Find a local radio station that broadcasts emergency information

A first aid kit should be part of your family's disaster plan.

You should also have the following disaster items on hand at all times:

- Flashlights and extra batteries
- Portable battery-operated radio
- First aid kit and first aid manual
- Boards, nails, and tape—to cover up your home's windows
- Plastic milk containers for emergency water storage
- Emergency food, such as canned food
- A non-electric can opener
- Sturdy shoes

Monitor the progress of a hurricane closely by tuning in to local television or radio forecasts. You can also call the National Hurricane Hotline at 1-900-410-NOAA to hear a recorded announcement of the latest hurricane advisory. Following are advisories you may hear when a hurricane has been sighted in your area.

Hurricane Watch

The National Hurricane Center issues a hurricane watch when a hurricane is expected to make landfall within 24 to 36 hours. The area covered by a hurricane watch is usually fairly large, as forecasters have not been able to determine exactly where the hurricane will strike. If you live in an area that is included in a hurricane watch, you should expect to get some bad weather even if the hurricane does not strike close by.

Hurricane Warning

As the hurricane moves closer to the coast, the National Hurricane Center issues a hurricane warning for a more specific area than that covered by the watch. At this point, an evacuation of coastal and low-lying areas may be ordered. If you live in an area to be evacuated, you should expect to be hit by the hurricane. Even if the area isn't experiencing hurricane-force winds, the warning may stay in effect if dangerously high water or a combination of high water and high waves are present.

The more that scientists learn about hurricanes and their movements, the better able they will be to warn people where and when hurricanes will strike. This will give people who live along the coast and in low-lying areas more time to seek shelter, and a better chance of surviving one of nature's most deadly weather forms.

GLOSSARY

air pressure The weight of air in the atmosphere pressing down at any one spot.

condensation The process where water vapor cools and becomes a liquid.

Coriolis effect A force that causes the wind to curve as a result of the Earth's rotation.

cyclonic motion Circular movement of air.

evacuate To order people to leave an area immediately because it is unsafe.

evaporate To change from a liquid to a gas.

eye An area of low pressure that forms the clear, calm core of a hurricane.

eye wall An area of thunderclouds that rotate around the hurricane's eye. It is where the heaviest rains fall and the strongest winds occur.

flash flooding A flood resulting from a large amount of rain falling in a short period of time.

humidity The amount of measured water in the air.

hurricane A tropical cyclone with sustained winds above 74 miles per hour.

hurricane warning A warning that hurricane-force winds are expected in a specific area within 24 hours.

hurricane watch An announcement that hurricane conditions pose a possible threat to an area within 36 hours.

meteorologist A scientist who studies weather and weather forecasting.

National Weather Service A government agency responsible for observing and forecasting weather.

Northern Hemisphere The half of the Earth located north of the equator.

seawall A wall that protects a coastal area from the force of ocean waves.

Southern Hemisphere The half of the Earth located south of the equator.

spin down The process by which a hurricane stops its spinning motion.

spiral rainbands Circular-moving bands of clouds accompanied by heavy showers and hurricane-force winds.

steering winds A combination of winds, including trade winds and prevailing westerlies, that steer a hurricane.

storm surge A dome of ocean water 50 to 100 miles wide, sometimes topped by waves.

thunderclouds Puffy, gray clouds that usually produce storms.

tornado A rapidly spinning column of air that comes into contact with the ground.

trade winds Winds near the equator that blow constantly in one direction. In the Northern Hemisphere, the trade winds blow from the East.

tropical cyclone A weather system that forms over the warm waters of tropical oceans and has a defined circular motion.

tropical depression The second stage of a developing hurricane. A storm accompanied by a drop in air pressure and rotating winds of 38 miles per hour or less.

tropical disturbance A moving cluster of thunderclouds with a center of low pressure. It is the first stage of a hurricane.

tropical storm A tropical cyclone where winds circle at speeds of 39 to 73 miles per hour around a low-pressure center. It is the last stage before a hurricane develops.

typhoon A tropical cyclone of hurricane strength occurring in the western and north Pacific Ocean.

water vapor Water in the form of a gas.

FOR FURTHER READING

Allaby, Michael. *Hurricanes.* New York: Facts on File, Inc., 1997.

Atkinson, Stuart. *Storms and Hurricanes: Understanding Geography Series.* Tulsa, OK: EDC Publishing, 1996.

Barber, Nicola. *Hurricanes and Storms.* North Pomfret, VT: Trafalgar Square Publishers, 1996.

Burroughs, William J. et al. *Nature Company Guides: Weather.* Alexandria, VA: Time-Life Books, 1996.

Robinson, Andrew. *Earth Shock.* New York: Thames & Hudson, 1993.

Sherrow, Victoria. *Hurricane Andrew: Nature's Rage.* Springfield, NJ: Enslow Publishers, 1998.

Souza, Dorothy M. *Hurricanes.* Minneapolis: Lerner Publications, 1994.

RESOURCES

National Weather Service
NWS Office of Public Affairs
1325 East-West Highway
Room 18454
Silver Spring, MD 20910
Web site: http://www.nws.noaa.gov

WEB SITES

National Hurricane Center
Everything you need to know about hurricanes, plus up-to-date tracking information.
http://www.nhc.noaa.gov/index

Hurricane Hunters Homepage
Information about Hurricane Hunters, plus take a virtual tour as a plane flies into the eye of a hurricane.
http://www.hurricanehunters.com

NASA's Hurricane Site for Kids
Includes facts about tropical twisters, plus a virtual tour of a hurricane.
http://kids.mtpe.hq.nasa.gov/hurricane/index.html

Hurricane and Natural Disaster Brochures
Online brochures produced by the National Ocean and Atmospheric Administration and the National Weather Service.
http://www.aoml.noaa.gov/general/lib/hurricbro.html

Index

A
air, 10, 12, 13, 14, 15, 28
Air Force Reserve, 37
air pressure, 9, 13, 19, 22
American Red Cross, 38
Atlantic Ocean, 9, 17
atmosphere, 11, 15, 36

C
clouds, 9, 12, 20, 21, 36
        cirrus clouds, 21
computers, 36
condensation, 12
Coriolis effect, 11, 13, 24
cyclones, 9
cyclonic wind, 10, 14

D
damage, 4, 20, 24, 27, 30,
        35
deaths, hurricane-related,
        21, 24, 28
destruction, 4, 38

E
Earth, 11, 36
energy, 7, 10, 24, 27
equator, 11, 22, 24
evacuation, 36, 38, 41
evaporation, 12
exhaust, 13, 14

eye wall, 19, 21, 22, 24
eye, 7, 19, 20, 21, 22, 37

F
flooding, 4, 24, 27, 28
Florida, 4, 20, 28, 38
forecast, 35, 37, 38, 40

G
Galveston, Texas, 29, 30

H
heat, 10, 12
humidity, 10
Hurricane Agnes, 28
Hurricane Andrew, 4, 28
Hurricane Hunters, 37-38

L
low pressure, 9, 10, 13, 14,
        19, 21, 29

M
meteorologists, 36, 38

N
National Hurricane Center,
        40, 41
National Hurricane Hotline,
        40
National Weather Service, 17
Northern hemisphere, 11,
        22

P
Pacific Ocean, 9

R
radar, 36
rain, 4, 12, 21, 22, 27, 28, 29

S
Saffir-Simpson scale, 32, 33
satellite, 35, 36
seawall, 30
shelters, 38, 41
shore, 4
south Pacific, 9
Southern hemisphere, 11
spin down, 24
spiral rainbands, 19, 21
storm surges, 27, 28-32
storm system, 8, 10, 11, 23
storm, 4, 7, 9, 10, 12, 13, 14, 15, 19, 20, 21, 22, 24, 27, 28, 30, 35, 36, 38
summer, 7

T
temperature, 12, 13, 19, 36
thunderclouds, 9, 21
thunderstorm, 10, 14
tides, 29
tornadoes, 4, 7, 22, 24
tropical cyclone, 7, 8, 9

tropical depression, 9
tropical disturbance, 9
tropical oceans, 4, 7
tropical storm, 9, 17, 35
typhoon, 9

U
United States, 4, 17, 32, 35, 38

W
warnings, 20
water vapor, 12
waves, 4, 21, 29, 32, 41
Weather Reconnaissance Squadron, 37
weather system, 7
weather, 4, 9, 17, 20, 24, 30, 36, 37, 41
wind speeds, 8, 22, 23, 28, 32, 37
wind, 4, 7, 9, 10, 11, 13, 15, 21, 24, 27, 29, 36
    prevailing westerlies, 22
    steering winds, 22, 23
    trade winds, 22
World Meteorological Association, 17

Credits

About the Author
Dean Galiano is a freelance writer. He lives in New York City.

Photo Credits
Cover, Title Page ©Kevin Vandivier/Vesti; p. 5 ©Alan Band/Tony Stone; pp. 6-7 ©Raymond Gehman/Corbis; pp. 16-17 ©Erik Schaffer/Corbis/Ecoscene; pp. 18-19 ©Warren Faidley/International Stock; p. 25 ©Rich Iwasaki/Tony Stone; pp. 26-27 ©Corbis/AFP; p. 30 ©Corbis; p. 31 ©Tony Stone; pp. 34-35 ©Imons, Chip/FPG; p. 37 ©Corbis/The Mariner's Museum; p. 39 ©Robert Reiff; pp. 11, 12, 14 Illustrations by Lisa Quattlebaum.

Cover Design
Kim M. Sonsky

Book Design and Layout
Lisa Quattlebaum

Consulting Editors
Mark Beyer and Jennifer Ceaser